The Derelict Heart

The Derelict Heart

Poems by Don Gutteridge

For Colin
with best wishes.
Don

First Edition

Hidden Brook Press
www.HiddenBrookPress.com
writers@HiddenBrookPress.com

The Derelict Heart
Don Dutteridge

Cover Design – Richard M. Grove
Layout and Design – Richard M. Grove
Cover Image – Bullstar/Shutterstock, by permission

Typeset in Garamond
Printed and bound in Canada
Distributed in USA by Ingram,
            in Canada by Hidden Brook Distribution

Library and Archives Canada Cataloguing in Publication

Title: The derelict heart / poems by Don Gutteridge.
Names: Gutteridge, Don, 1937- author.
Identifiers: Canadiana (print) 20200360965
            Canadiana (ebook) 20200361007
ISBN 9781989786161 (softcover)
ISBN 9781989786178 (ebook)
Classification: LCC PS8513.U85 D47 2020
            DDC C811/.54—dc23

For Tim, James and Kevin,
and for Tom in loving memory.

Table of Contents

– The Silence Between the Stars – *p. 1*
– Gran – *p. 2*
– Perfection – *p. 3*
– Comng Home Lonely – *p. 4*
– Bardic – *p. 5*
– Joys – *p. 6*
– Untugged – *p. 7*
– Riches – *p. 8*
– Rhapsody – *p. 9*
– Cribbed – *p. 10*
– Derby – *p. 11*
– Solo – *p. 12*
– Gleam – *p. 13*
– Elapse – *p. 14*
– Dance – *p. 15*
– Chime – *p. 16*
– Tropes – *p. 17*
– Ghosts – *p. 18*
– Itch – *p. 19*
– Green and Growing – *p. 20*
– Bard – *p. 21*
– Companions – *p. 22*
– "I Can't Breathe" – *p. 23*
– Gardens – *p. 24*
– Silver Spoon – *p. 25*
– Enraptured – *p. 26*
– Surmise – *p. 27*
– Budding – *p. 28*
– Inch – *p. 29*
– Type – *p. 30*
– Perseverance – *p. 31*
– Easter – *p. 32*

– Gift – *p. 33*
– Hymn – *p. 34*
– Biblical – *p. 35*
– Dialogue – *p. 36*
– Celibate – *p. 37*
– Rude – *p. 38*
– Bolt – *p. 39*
– Forge – *p. 40*
– Glance – *p. 41*
– Daughters – *p. 42*
– Dance – *p. 43*
– High and Dry – *p. 44*
– Temerity – *p. 45*

Forty-One for Tom

– Parlance – *p. 47*
– Humdrum – *p. 48*
– Writ on Water – *p. 49*
– Rollers – *p. 50*
– Radium – *p. 51*
– Too Beautiful – *p. 52*
– Somewhere – *p. 53*
– In Place of Tears – *p. 54*
– Untroubled – *p. 55*
– Renewal – *p. 56*
– Tom – *p. 57*
– Imperishable – *p. 58*
– Walking the Woods – *p. 59*
– Remembering – *p. 60*
– Tom's Song, Again – *p. 61*

– Foolish – *p. 62*
– Deep – *p. 63*
– Immortal – *p. 64*
– Bud the Spud – *p. 65*
– Precincts – *p. 66*
– Comng Home Lonely – *p. 67*
– Home-Things – *p. 68*
– No Guarantees – *p. 69*
– Dionysian – *p. 70*
– Grotto – *p. 71*
– A Memory – *p. 72*
– Gift – *p. 73*
– Fictive – *p. 74*
– Old Saw – *p. 75*
– Autumnal – *p. 76*
– Adroit – *p. 77*
– Lalling – *p. 78*
– Never – *p. 79*
– Bereavement – *p. 80*
– Precambrian: Cyprus Lake – *p. 81*
– Passion – *p. 82*
– Seesawing – *p. 83*
– Rush – *p. 84*
– Buoyancy – *p. 85*
– Song – *p. 86*

Twenty-Eight for Anne

– When the Dream Ends – *p. 98*
– Where No Light Goes – *p. 99*
– Alive and Loving – *p. 90*
– Unforsaken – *p. 91*
– Bouquet – *p. 92*
– Roses – *p. 93*

– Alight – *p. 94*
– The Far Side of the Dark – *p. 95*
– Possible – *p. 96*
– Tap-Dance – *p. 97*
– Pristine – *p. 98*
– In the Bone – *p. 99*
– Cruise – *p. 100*
– Soft and Low – *p. 101*
– Ritual – *p. 102*
– Whistle – *p. 103*
– Distance – *p. 104*
– Tingling – *p. 105*
– Condoning – *p. 106*
– Stark – *p. 107*
– Oddity – *p. 108*
– Still – *p. 109*
– At Ease – *p. 110*
– Embarcation – *p. 111*
– Big Town – *p. 112*
– Where Love Abides – *p. 113*
– No Ending – *p. 114*
– Night After Night – *p. 115*
– When the Dark is Light Enough – *p. 116*
– On Honeymoon Bay – *p. 117*

About the Author – *p. 119*

The Silence Between the Stars

In the gloaming over the River
flats (where we sometimes
flew our kites in the big-
breathed wind from the lake),
we played squat-tag
or May I? while the moon
loomed above our random
roaming and threw its mottled
light our way, while we waited
for the sky to darken and ignite
the silence between the stars.

Gran

For my grandmother in loving memory

Whenever I think of you
(and it is more than once
in a new moon), I recall
the aroma of apple pie
adrift on a Sunday morning
or lemon Jello cooling
on the back verandah or a woman
forever aproned, where I burrowed
into a festoon of feathers,
and I remember, too, the lavender
perfume of your quilted bed-
chamber and the click of your change-
purse with a nickel nibbling
my palm, and you and Grandpa
coupled for life, your love
a soothing symmetry, rocking
away a summer's evening
on the side porch, *The Observer*
fluttering at your chin like bride's
bandanna, and I try not to think
about your final face
in that copper coffin,
your smile a grim rictus,
your eyes, that would never glow
again, shut against the world's
will, and me.

Perfection

After Emily Dickinson

Missus Bray spent
each May morning
grazing in her garden among
the flowers she bustled into bloom
to ease the wince of her widow-
hood, and every petal
had to grow just so,
as if perfection were hers
to reach.

Comng Home Lonely

Coming home lonely
to a house that echoes when I wake it,
my mother migrained in her room,
father gone as usual,
brother seeking solace
further down the road
and, undisturbed, I batten
on a book, let my fancy
free, find a parched
page avid for ink,
and pen my first poem.

Bardic

When I was just young,
I stepped into Spring and the mists
of morning like Adam complicit
with Eden, lustrous with light
(where crocuses bulged in mustard
aarray and tulips bled
as red as a ripened rose
and the earth under them oozed
tubers) and I trod the serene
green of Grandfather's lawn
like Jesus cruising Galilee,
my head swollen Pentecostal
with poems and ribald rhymes,
and I thanked the gods of this
incelibate season and passed
my day: bibbed Bardic
and lost in Paradisal ease.

Joys

In Grandfather's yard
I said a welcome to crocuses
in their labial lustre
and tulips dipped in menstrual
red and lilies lit
with swallowed light and rose-
buds in tumescent fettle
and wild iris with nettled
stamens and pistoning pistils
and in the eaves above
starlings remarked on the merits
of the day and sparrows gossiped
on the gables and it was all
my delight to sit me down
and compose a poem to celebrate
the urgent surges of such
a Spring and the joys it leaves
unbroken.

Untugged

I was almost twelve before
I ventured into the big beyond
that squeezed my village and kept me
hugging home all
those incubating years,
where I grew in wombed degrees
and let the poems percolate
from Foster's Pond or the sands
of Canatara, and I felt like Jesus
ambling easy on Galilee,
my head singing biblical
with psalms and Parnassian parables
and I was content to remain
there, untuggd by Time
like a fly in amber, the ink
of my childhood drying
on the page.

Riches

When I was a boy in breeches,
I stepped out into the misted
morning and said "Hello"
to Spring, when buds nudged
and Grandma's tulips ripped
airward and bled beauty,
and forsythia, scissored by sun,
bloomed anyway, and I walked
upon the town like Adam
aroused in Eden, rinsed
in innocence, miming his Maker
and pressing every edible
object into the pincers of a poem —
rupturing reason and begetting
bedlam, and I've known
since that paradisal day
that my life would abound
with the riches of rhyme.

Rhapsody

The morning sun rises
out of First Bush and pours
its molten marigold
down Michigan Ave,
shrivelling shadow in ell
and alley, burnished with liquid
light, and around them
a village quickens and children,
freed from dreaming, lope
and linger in their vehement voyaging,
and in the milkweed meadow
a stone's throw from grand-
father's home, where a lark
sings solo and Monarchs
tip-toe on prickled pouches
with their silken secret, a solitary
rhymester rhapsodizes
under a sky too blue
to be beautiful.

Cribbed

Miss McDonald made
a writer out of me,
praising the story I'd cribbed
from the class Reader, but the words
were all mine, rising
from some liberated nub
inside like a dew-winged
bird, unfazed
by the perils of the page or the rigours
of rhyme, and I swallowed Parnassus
whole, knowing even
then that poetry is the soul
singing to itself.

Derby

My pal Wiz confected
a go-cart out of orange
crates and abandoned buggy-
wheels, and I pushed him
up and down the town,
pausing to accept the polite
applause of bystanders,
and when Herbie Gilbert
rolled past in his Tin
Lizzie, he saluted us
with his ooga-ooga horn
and we felt like born-again
winners in the Soap-Box
Derby.

Solo

I saw her there but once
and that was more than enough:
Marybelle Cooper
curled on the sun-strummed
sands of Canatara
in her one-piece suit,
clinging to her girlish curves
like a lover's ruffling hands,
and I spent the rest of my day
humming without pause
like Orpheus on his lute, and singing
solo to Cupid's apt
applause.

Gleam

When Jo- dropped her panties
and exposed the prize between
her thighs, she had a gleam
in her eye like Delilah's snipping
Samson's lofty locks,
like Salome's doing her death-
dance unfrocked,
like Bathsheba's dithering David,
or like Eve's outwitting Adam
with an ample apple, and what
I want to know is did they
enjoy the triumph of their titillation?

Elapse

Marybelle Cooper,
my best friend's cousin,
stood behind the white
picket fence that hugged
our yard in her Tartan sweater
under which her just—
about breasts breathed
serenely, and when she smiled
my way, all the sonnets
I longed to sing lapsed
on my lips and when she smiled
again, something tugged me
aside and I knew for the first
time what love was.

Dance

When evening came down
upon our village, we ran
headlong into the gloaming
to play our home-grown
ritual games, and in season
and out and fancy-free,
we found new reasons
to rhyme, and like any other
Medieval town, we also
danced and kept our time.

Chime

Shirley doing the can-can
under the Parisian trees
on grandfather's lawn:
all soothing thighs
and nubile knees and,
aiming to please with a
glint in her eye like Eve's
ogling the apple, she chimes:
"I lift my leg so high
you can see my cherry
pie ai ai!"
and we all wake up
in China.

Tropes

I was told the first word
I uttered was "No!", as if
I were warning the world of my arrival
and wouldn't take "no"
for an answer, a one-word
poem in hopes of establishing
my bona fides, and soon
I got the knack of nouns,
the vim of verbs and the rigour
of rhyme, and these were the tropes
a poet could drown in.

Ghosts

Everywhere I look in the
noonday dazzle or under
the slow moon of a summer
evening, I see the ghosts
of those who touched and left
their tender trace: my grand-
father who lived for three
years in the trenches and then
lived again and Gran
aglow in the smiles of the littl'uns
tugging her apron and Uncle
Potsy who loved me until
I grew to love him and my Dad
who skated as smooth as a swan
polishing a pond, whom
I forgave the itch of his addiction
and a host of others: boy-
hood chums and village
vassals who peopled my life
and imperfect poems, who let me
hug the world home.

Itch

O it's hard not to be
immortal, for when we are gone,
we live on in the memories
of those who loved us alive
and in the stories they tell
of us when day draws down
and we become part of the lore
that thrives wherever there are
humans with an itch for history,
and so it is, I look upon
my demise with no regard
for endings, compromise
or polite applause, certain
that, against the odds,
the long sentence, my life,
will not be periodic.

Green and Growing

If it's Spring in the Point,
the lilacs on grandfather's
hedge are livid with light
and there is bulb-burst
and fledgling fusion and juiced
buds anointed in the sun's
nuzzle, and I find myself
meandering the milkweed meadow
with a thirst for everything green
and growing, and the air aloft
is soft with the singing of larks
and the drone of home-going
bees, and I have such a
longing to pull the perfect
poem out of blood and bone.

Bard

I find it hard to imagine
a life without the wizardry
of words: the nuances of nouns
and verbs surging: pinned
in the prism of a poem, where rhyme
has its reasons and rhythm is what
the heart hears in the silence
between beats and simile
has its seasons, and I was born
to pain and poetry, and longed
to embrace the arcane business
of being a bard.

Companions

For Colm O'Sullivan in Memoriam

You and I were golfing
companions in our halcyon days
when the sun shone down
upon us and our fairways
as bright as an Irish smile,
and I loved to watch you amble
ahead, rotund and risible,
with a twinkle in your Kerryman's eye
and a gambler's urge to drive
your innocent orb into the
next county and make
your irons sing while lofting
the ball greenward, where,
with a nod to the golfing gods
you sink a ten-footer
and the gallery, charmed by your Gaelic
guile, applauds.

"I Can't Breathe"

For George Floyd

While the world watched, a man
with a heart harried by hatred,
knelt upon your neck
in a parody of prayer, deaf
to your plea: "I can't breathe!",
a phrase unfurled like a beacon
of outrage and carried
to far continents, wherever
men and women looked
to love to turn the page
on racial violence, and some-
where, miles from the nearest
bigot, you: looking down
and forgiving, your eyes wreathed
in smiles.

Gardens

In the milkweed meadow
a stone's throw from grand-
father's yard in the sizzle
of summer, butterflies flutter
at ease on the afternoon breeze,
bees, peregrinating
from flower to flower, nosh
on nectar and, high above,
a lark soars with song,
and I am welcomed into
this paradisal place
as one of the Elect, and I pull
open a plump pod
with its silken secret like Jesus
breaking bread before
the Apostles, and I say a prayer
to the god who fashioned such
gardens for our innocent use.

Silver Spoon

Contrary to popular view,
my grandfather held
his knife in the left hand
and his fork in the other,
and just free from my silver
spoon, I took to cutlery
like a duck to a reed-rife
pond, with left-hand-
knife and right hand-
fork, and oddly enough
we soon grew fond.

Enraptured

When I was young enough
to know better, my world
was hedged by grandfather's
lilacs, lavish in morning
light, and an arbor hung
with roses, and I roamed the village
beyond like Adam idling
in Eden or an ardent Argo,
welcomed by the sea-warm
womb of an archipelago
until I met the edge
of the everywhere I called
home, free from Time's
tyranny and happy as a poet
enraptured by rhyme.

Surmise

For Tom and for in loving memory

You were the love-child
we never had, the star-
lit delight of our lives,
and when your blue eyes
stared up at me
for the first time, my heart
surprised itself with wild
jolts of joy, and we watched
you grow from callow youth
to muscular man, our own
hopes coupled with the dreams
you dreamed of yourself
and we shared the pain that,
at the end, grew too big
to be borne, and grieve
that you cannot come to us
again with your wise surmise.

Budding

We were just friends
gathered in Hendrie's hen-
house, and when Jo-
began admiring her brand-
new breasts with their stippled
nipples and then dropped
her pants to expose the shy
surprise between her thighs,
my eyes widened at the rush
of blood somewhere
below: the first budding
of desire.

Inch

I seasoned my village with poems
where rhyme has its reasons,
metaphors move and similes
sing, and I willed myself
to catalogue its Dickensian
denizens and their epic follies,
to stipple in stout stanzas
those days when Time
unwinched its grip,
and canonize Canatara's
immaculate sands, and I felt
as if could ride off
any horizon and still
be an inch from home.

Type

In Hendrie's hen-house,
anything goes, where the girls,
exposing the ripe rose
furled in their thighs' vise,
make the boys blush
as crimson as a crushed anemone,
and one of them, suspecting
my erection, pipes up
and says, "You're not my type!"

Perseverance

For Bob Clark

We watch, awe-struck,
as you break your maiden on Hickory
Ridge, taking sixteen
stiff-whiffing practice
strokes and then, back
bent like a fresh pretzel,
you send the ball looping
leftward over a ploughed
field like a dying duck,
and in the certainty that history
does not repeat itself,
you fix your eye upon
a far horizon, pluck up
your pluck and begin again.

Easter

In my village, May was the
cruellist month, when tulips
erupted voluptuous and crocuses
cleaved a crotch of loam,
licked lascivious by lancing
light, and lilacs bloom
bridal and high above
crows careened in the wind's
welter, a season's winging
remembered in their genes, and larks
levitate, their trembling tune
teasing the breeze, and down
below, a caterpillar,
uncocooned, weaves
and worries, embossing
a lactic leaf, and an adder
seesaws through a tickle
of grass, and Spring comes
helter-skelter to town,
tantalizing our tillage,
and it's Easter again and time
to justify Jesus, notched
on His cross.

Gift

In the morning of my boyhood
the sun stood above
First Bush like a stunned
doubloon, where robins
throbbed with song and adders
seethed in the grass, and I erupted
from grandfather's house
like a butterfly from its home cocoon
and hallooed my village like Adam
seizing Eden and uttered
a prayer to the gods who gave me
this gracious ground
and the gift of language to glorify it
in poem and story.

Hymn

For Anne and for Tom in loving memory

I've spent more than a life-
time inking the world
with poems and stories, and you
have so enthused my Muse
that words flow to the
pristine page as if
delivered from a brimming of my breath,
but when you left me bereft,
I limned a lyric alive,
a dolorous hymn to what
has been lost, and I came
at last to the brink, looked
over and then up,
and for what seemed like an age
I uncoupled, but love
is more diligent than Death
and we all survived.

Biblical

The sun rose over
First Bush each
summer morning like an
old-testament prophet,
like Elijah and his chariot of fire,
and I was Bible-bred,
teething on its stories: Adam
ungrieving in Eden,
David and his potent pebble,
Moses cleaving the Red Sea,
Samson with his liberated locks
(his eyes gouged out on Gaza),
Daniel flouting lions
in their den and Zacharias
trembling in his tree,
waiting for the Messiah, and my mind
seethed with such Promethean
parables (as I weighed the wages
of sin) and I grew a story-
grammar I'll pursue until
my last poem perishes
on the page.

Dialogue

My poems are a dialogue between
me and myself, and I sing
sonnets to civility, ballads
to my beloved, some gist
caught up in a couplet,
quatrains rife with rhyme,
and when I speak, I wax
iambic, happy to be
in this long conversation,
my life.

Celibate

Each summer morning
the sun boiled out of
First Bush and lashed
my village with lacquered light,
and I greeted its streets like Adam
poaching Paradise and rousted
Butch and Bones and Wiz
to reconnoitre every ell
and alley, all the way
to my boyhood beach, where,
at last, and to no-one's surprise,
I found myself alone
and celibate: with an itch for history
and a passion for poetry.

Rude

God in His oddity fashioned
Eve to be Adam's companion,
and all was well until Eve
feasted on the forbidden fruit
and they knew their nakedness,
a conjugal couple rudely
nude in a fallen world
with a newly-gained passion
for pain and poetry

Bolt

They say that lightning never
strikes the same tree
twice, but in the summer
when I was almost me,
both of the maples that hugged
grandfather's house
and shaded my boyhood
games were struck down
by a single savage bolt,
and the home where I was lavished
by love and jolted with joy
and which I spun into a
dozen pulsing poems
and ringing rhymes, stood
there shivering in the sunshine
like a prude nude, and I knew
then that nothing is ever
the same again.

Forge

O the gorgeous girls
of Canatara! I see
their elongated bodies softening
in the sand, their one-piece
suits colluding with their curves,
while the boys, too shy
to give it a try, are content
to be furled in the forge
of desire.

Glance

O Nancy Mara, you were
the belle of Canatara!
I see you still in your blue
one-piece suit,
seducing those Saharan
sands with your lithe-limbed
beauty, and later on
stroking the bevelled swells
of our mutual Lake with silken
symmetry, and I would forgo
my share of the world's luck
for a single glance meant
just for me (and enough
pluck to return it).

Daughters

When I was young enough
to know better and still
in the gist of boyhood, I looked
at the girls around me with a
particular interest:
Nancy Mara to whom I took
an immaculate fancy;
Shirley McCord with her high-
stepping strut between
teasing twirls of baton;
Grace Leckie, two
rows over with breasts
breathing through wool;
Judy Hammond waving
Hello with a long-legged lope;
and Marybelle Cooper,
the girl next door
who lit the wick of my desire:
Daughters of Eve one
and all, who took the fall
for mankind and the insights
of an apple and the illicit pleasures
of conjugal joy.

Dance

When evening came down
upon our village, we ran
headlong into the gloaming
to play our home-grown
ritual games, and in season
and out and fancy-free,
we found new reasons
to rhyme, and like any other
Medieval town, we also
danced and kept our time.

High and Dry

Before morning broke
first upon the world,
the Great Poetaster
bespoke his one-word
poem into the Void and Earth
rose up from the cleaved
seas with tidbits parcelled
out for Paradise and the greenery
of Eden, and Adam, newly
nude, was inked in innocence
and Eve burst full-
bodied from a ribald rib,
and as the seasons passed
in succinct exactitude, all
was well in God's arrogant
eye until Eve took Him
to the brink and ambushed an apple,
leaving mankind high
and dry.

Temerity

Adam was our first versifier,
naming the flora and fauna
of Eden's green demesnes
with terse temerity as the
sylvan syllables sang
on his tongue, and when Eve
brought him an arrayed bouquet
he chimed the blooms one
by one into an ode to her chastity
and their ungendered abode
and the seasons passed with an easy
effort until Eve questioned
the reasons for rhymes and began
iambicizing on her own
and the wannabe bards soon
wrote themselves out of
the perfumed precincts of Paradise.

Forty for Tom

In loving memory

Parlance

You were the champion of my Point
Edwardian poems, a sympathetic
ear when the Muse demurred,
and my voice was amplified
by your steadfast fidelity
to all things Bardic, and I recall
the first words to come un-
hampering out from a head
already singing with syllables
and infant iambics, and I dreamed
you would take a star-turn
at soothsaying similes,
a fellow traveller on the green
pastures of Parnassus,
each of us anointed, redeemed
by the Dionysian dance
of poetry and parlance —

                              but now
you are gone into that nether
night and, with you, all
the poems you'll never write.

Humdrum

We spent one Sunday
morning in that book-nook
we called our inner sanctum
discussing how I was born
biblical: took to Jesus
and His rolled stone and Peter
combing Galilee's shore
to be dubbed a Fisher of Men
and Elijah's sublime climb
to Heaven and Moses born
in a basket and suborning seas
and David with his impertinent pebble
and Samson, bibbed in blood,
collapsing columns — ,
and when you asked me
if I believed these outsized
fabrications, I paused before
saying, "Of course, they livened
up my humdrum days,"
and you grinned in bemused
reply, and something
passed between us that lasted
until the good God
of my childhood let you die.

Writ on Water

You were my Right Reader,
parsing my poems with a gentle
Jeremiad, letting
the lush larceny of verse
move you with its iambic ambling
and you navigated my fiction
like a seagoing Drake,
your literary radar pitch
perfect, your sensibility
as fine-tuned as a Muse's
daughter, and now that you
are gone, I wake each
meagre morning to write
these words, like Keats,
on water.

Rollers

In this dream we are strolling
the moonlit sands of Canatara
and out in the Lake wavelets
breed slow rollers
that bathe our unshod
feet, and I show you
the dunes where I played away
my Saturday afternoons
and where Attawandaron
came to glorify their gods,
and we agree that this inland
sea is hallowed ground
like Galilee where Jesus
walked on water with infinite
ease and Peter deified
as Fisher of Men, and I do not
wish to wake and find
that you have died.

Radium

You and I slow-
rowing over Cameron,
our oars dimpling the surface,
and we are hugged by ante-
diluvian forests of spruce
and pine and birch
(with bark as alabaster as a
nun's wimple), and we
are rinsed by the sun's radium,
silence in the blue above
and silence in the precincts below
(where perch peregrinate and minnows
Wrinkle) and we are happy
to find such un-
encumbered joy in simple
things and pass our days
content with our lot, tugged
by love.

Too Beautiful

What I'll remember most
are the lazy afternoons
we spent in the heat-haze
angling for perch on Cameron's
blue lagoon or trolling
for the lunkers who lay in wait
in the dappled dells below
and the grin you gave me
when the big bass bit
that glowed like a day-time
moon, and I need the embers
of these memories now
that you have gone and left me
to dream what might have been,
knowing all along
that I must forgive you
your going, that you were too
beautiful to live.

Somewhere

When the gods let your body
be, I almost believed
in their benignity, and I would have
marshalled the stars and summoned
the sun or hitched a lift
to the moon to keep you alive
and loving among us, unsuccumbed,
riding the itch of your addiction,
bringing balm to the beasts
of field and fallow with your vet's
touch, and when you came
to the brink of your breath, and yielded,
somewhere in the world
a light winked out.

In Place of Tears

In place of tears, I turn
to your podcasts and once
more we are in our mutual
room, snug among books
and matters literary, and I wanted
your life to be a perpetual
poem, full of years
and the solace of sonnets and Shakespeare
and home-truths: replete
with sturdy sons and fetching
daughters, your grandchildren
miming the words I penned
in the bold hope the gods,
in their grace, would look upon
me kindly and let you
grow old.

Untroubled

We stroll through the elderly
oaks of Canatara
and I show you where we played
cops-and-robbers and the refreshment
stand with double-dip
for a dime, and the afternoon
softens around us and we leave
the park and its lofted trees
and amble onto the dunes,
seething with sunlight
and older than Methusaleh's muse,
and we lob our bodies upon
the bevelled warmth and sense
the heat of centuries burning
through like banked fire
or rarefied runes, and then
at last the Great Lake
looms like Jehovah's Deep
when the world invented
itself new, and Noah
gambled all on an ark,
and I want this day,
like you, to live forever,
untroubled by anything
as dire as dying.

Renewal

I wish one more time
to bring you back to Cameron
and see it renewed in your child's
eyes, and take you fishing
once again like Peter
on the shores of Galilee,
waiting for Jesus to seize
his soul, and we, too,
had our miracle moments on that
miniature inland sea,
incubating bass in its blue
dells for our pleasure, and I
remember well your maiden
catch and the look you gave me
when the big-mouth hooked:
lit with love and wild
with surmise.

Tom

There is no bottom to my grief,
your passing has left me
with half a heart, I cannot
bear to think of the pain
that must have pierced you at the end,
your life but partly lived
with so much achieved
and promises pending; I was there
at your borning and loved you even
then with a fierce felicity,
and O how I hoped to see you
thrive for a thousand autumns,
grow as old as I
and flame out with a flourish
that would stun the stars.

Imperishable

I cherish this photo
of you seated on your little
red truck like an over-zealous
fire chief, with a smile
that says, "Look out world,
here I come!" and now
that you've left us numb
with grief at a life half-
lived and your luck run out,
I still have this imperishable
photo of a smiling boy
on his little red truck.

Walking the Woods

Tom and I walking
the woods above Cyprus,
a bright breeze lapping
the birch leaves, rippling
wild orchids at our feet,
setting a hawk adrift
in the high sky, while blue
jays argue about trees
and perches and the afternoon
ambles on, and we are happy
merely to be taking the right
fork in our road, knowing
that the good gods in their
elevated eyrie approve
our duo-dallying, and that love
is deeper than dying.

Remembering

I remember your first smile
(Grandma said it was gas)
and the morning you crawled
across the carpet, legs
and arms serendipitous,
and the day you took a tentative
step, your body mastering
at last momentum, like a swimmer
welcomed by water, and the first
words to burst from your breath
like a poet's rhymes on a maiden
page, and I recall all
the birthdays, long walks
in the woods and afternoons
on Cameron's blue billowing,
and you made me feel as chuffed
as a drum major in a pipe
band until you made
a deal with Death, and as I ease
into my age, I can only pray
for a life that is ripe with remembering

Tom's Song, Again

Your lullaby lalling was so
sweet (your crib one
room from mine), I put it
into a poem to make its music
memorable, and now that you
are gone, I can reclaim
that syllabled song
and bring you singing back
to me no more than a
baby's breath away
and I want so much
to reach out and touch you
I would call "My dibs!" on Death.

Foolish

I hoped you would carry our name
into the next century,
marry and have four sons
(and a daughter to sweeten your age)
and our bloodline would prosper
in your gentle genes, and I
would have someone to peruse
my poems and read them aloud
to your children's children in front of
a hearth seasoned by serenity,
and tell them, to stir and amuse,
stories of a grandfather
foolish enough to love
without reason or reservation

Deep

When Lear, harrowed on a heath,
heard his fool say,
"Poor Tom's a-cold,"
I thought of you in your youth
hoping to grow old,
and I wanted you alive and loving
for keeps in the here
and now, but I am alone
with a grief as burrowed as bone
and as deep as its marrow.

Immortal

You come to me in dreams
as if you were too shy
to say goodbye, and we are
together once again
cavorting in Cameron's
minnowing shallows, jigging
for thin-finned pickerel
on a June afternoon
under skies seamless
with sunlight, netting
a big-mouth on a red-
letter day or walking
the woods above our Lake
where wild orchids blow
easy in the breeze, and I do
not wish to wake up
and find that you are not
immortal.

Bud the Spud

O how you loved your namesake,
Stompin' Tom Connors,
tormenting his floor-board
like a one-hoofed Flamenco
dancer and strumming his ten-
dollar guitar to ballads
born of hardscrabble
and dreaming a life beyond
Skinner's Pond and aching
for the fillip of fame, mapping
the villages and towns of his native
land with a people's poetry
and toe-tapping rhymes
in a voice like a down-home
Caruso or the crackle of the Doomsday
Gun, and you framed his inscribed
photo and hung it in your room
like a talisman, the last thing
you saw as you drifted to sleep,
humming Bud the Spud.

Precincts

I was there the day you were born,
O my beautiful boy,
taking your first brief
breaths in an incubator
like a specimen under glass,
with a pair of impassioned blue
eyes surprised by it all
and setting the room around you
a-bloom, if to say,
"Good morning, world,
I've just spent nine
months welded to a womb
and it's time you let me be me,"
and I felt myself perambulating
in the precincts of joy.

Comng Home Lonely

Coming home lonely
to a house that echoes when I wake it,
my mother migrained in her room,
father gone as usual,
brother seeking solace
further down the road
and, undisturbed, I batten
on a book, let my fancy
free, find a parched
page avid for ink,
and pen my first poem.

Home-Things

You wished to see the village
that spawned a million words,
and so we sojourned there
one municipal May morning
and trod the streets unleashed
in my poems and stories, and I
showed you grandfather's lawn
and the side walk with its "granny"
cracks, and pointed out
the room where my fancy took
fire and I was groomed
to be a writer, and you nodded
as if such home-things
really mattered, and I knew
then how much I wanted you
to live for a hundred seasons,
before the gods in their unreason
took you back.

No Guarantees

If I could bring you back
alive like Clyde Beatty
his Barnum and Bailey lions,
I would tell you how much
I enjoyed our angling for bass
on Cameron's placid blue,
letting the afternoon soften
around us or paddling
upstream on the way to Cyprus
through interlacing lilies
with blooms as saffron as Van
Gogh's ochre and butterflies
afloat on the buoyancy of the breeze
and a hummingbird strumming
the air with diaphanous wings
and a water-snake see-
sawing at ease, and I like
to think of your passing as a dream
I can interrupt at will,
but when the gods gave us
the gift of life, there were no
guarantees, and so I remain
here, mourning still
your abrupt uncoupling.

Dionysian

O how you loved your music!
You and I in the living room
conducting Beethoven's Fifth
like tempestuous Toscaninis,
waving our phantom batons
to the tympani's tantrum,
the sweet serve of violins,
the prancing of piccalos,
and, for a cerebral second,
our eyes harmonize
and our souls fuse as we
succumb to the Dionysian dance

Grotto

We walked to the Grotto over
rock that dinosaurs drummed on
and through woods where Attawandaron
stalked roe-buck
and bear, and a solstice sun
shrivelled our shadows in the odd
beaver-meadow among
tamarack and ferned fir
as a rattler gee'd and haw'd
across our track just
before The Grotto gleamed
ahead like a May morning
dreaming in Eden, livid
with light and brushed
frivolous by a breeze above
the ebb of an undertow,
(as pristine as a saint's shrine)
and I would give my soul
to the gods of gratuity if I could
take you there once
again, loving and whole,
and watch your eyes widen,
blue with wonder.

A Memory

For Joe Organ and Tom in loving memory

Grandpa watching Tom
and Joe a-swim in the university
pool: twelve-years
young and fused in a friendship
that would last half a lifetime:
Tom with his heft going
hand-over-hand as deft
as a dolphin and Joe, all
knees and elbows speeding
beside him as silken as a salmon
unbruised by rapids,
and I hold this memory
aloft and for a little
while the pain of my loss
is softened.

Gift

on listening to Tom's podcast

Once again I hear
your voice as if you were still
alive and we were settled
in that book-blessed nook,
discussing the passion of poetry
or the nuances of the novel,
and our conversation proceeded
with the ease of an April breeze,
and O how I wanted you
to thrive beyond your allotted
years and come to me
in fulsome fettle whenever
our love needed a gentle
renewing, and I could thank
the gracious gods again
for such a gift as you,
and rejoice.

Fictive

Now that you are gone
I stare at this drawing
you crayoned with your six-year
hand: you and I
seated in my uncle's row-
boat, fishing rods
at the ready (on Cameron,
I suppose, where there isn't
a breath of a breeze, we are steeped
in sunlight and where anything
like happiness goes), and one
of us is bearded below
a smudge of blue for sky
and the other has a tangerine
splash of hair above
a ripple of blue for water:
a child's fictive picturing
of two souls linked
in life, at ease with the other's
love.

Old Saw

You agreed with the old saw
that "golf is a good walk
spoiled," but we ventured out
anyways onto the groomed grass
of the Thames Valley links
on a soft June afternoon
and I watched in awe as you sent
that pebbled spheroid
lazily aloft with a succinct
swerve of your borrowed wedge
and I applauded as the ball garnished
the green and stopped on a dime
an elfin inch from the pin
and the grin you gave me
has lasted a lifetime.

Autumnal

All the willows in Gibbon's
Park are weeping at the thought
of your premature passing
and summer's leaves are gone,
like you, and November's breezes
blow autumnal in sympathizing
song and umber skies,
in mourning, darken, unlanced
by light, and I remember
well the baptism of your borning
and long to make you immortal
in the perpetual prism of a poem.

Adroit

On amber afternoons
Tom and I cavorted
in Cameron's shimmering shallows
like blue-finned dolphins
delighted with their own adroit
gymnastics, and we took turns
ducking under like cruising
loons, and Tom gave me
a gargantuan grin, as if
to say, "Such days
are a gift from the gods and we
are here, anointed," and I felt
a tug of love so strong
I wanted to hug him whole
and go perambulating to the moon.

Lalling

One room away
I heard you, curled
in your crib, lalling like a
Diva liberating her scales
and I was suddenly lashed
by love, and prayed you'd ferry
my genes far into the new
century, keep the blood-
line alive, immortalize
our name, but now you are gone,
my passionate plea mocked
by the gods, and I am left
to cope without the saving
solace of your smile, here
where no hope looms.

Never

Never again will we cavort
in Cameron's hallowed shallows
like unprincipled porpoises
or troll its green dells
for big-mouth bass
or jig its weeded desmesnes
for pickerel or let its sun
settle on us like an afternoon
snooze, and never again
will we sit in that book-
lined nook and have
our minds mingle melodiously
while we remark on the pithiness
of poetry or the gist of fiction
or the delightful drollery of our linked
lives, and never again
will I hear your soul sing.

Bereavement

You fought valiantly against
the odds and the itch of your addiction,
but the gods don't play fair:
they made you bright, kind,
loving and gifted but too
beautiful to live, leaving me
adrift with your death, and I will
remember the perfect pitch
of your grin until the last
breath bereaves my body.

Precambrian: Cyprus Lake

Tom and I pole
our way through the blue
isthmus that keeps our lakes
from hugging, where bullfrogs
plop from lily-pads
basted with bloom, and we debouch
into Cyprus with the morning sun
gleaming the lake pristine
and we drop our baited lines
into the dark dells below
and wait for the first terse
tug, and later on
in the soft sift of the afternoon
we stroll through the woods
to the north, where butterflies
flutter on wobbled wings
and orchids lie in shy
disguise and a rattler seesaws
across our path and blue
jays natter in the breeze
and we step at last free
of our shadows and come face
to face with the great "Grotto"
carved out of Precambrian cliff
and we look at one another
as if for the first time,
our love sealed in silence,
our thoughts aloft with the gods
who dreamed such a land.

Passion

You always loved animals,
you chucked our three kittens
under the chin just
to hear them purr, you laughed
at the panicked antics of our Scottie,
rode bareback on our malamute
like Roy Rogers straddling
his Palomino, settled a fretting
colt with a surgeon's subtle
touch, and so to no-one's
surprise you became a vet
and tamed the beasts of the field
like Orpheus with his soothing lute,
and now that you are gone
and we have yielded to grief,
we are left with the memories
of a wise-eyed boy
and the creatures he loved with a
poet's passion.

Seesawing

Tom and I in tender
tandem meandering the creek
that links our twinned lakes
and, too shallow for paddles
we pole along like Huck
Finns on holiday, lancing
Lily-pads where bull-
frogs swing on tiny
trapezes, with the blue bowl
of the sky above and the afternoon
sun sifting down like a
summertime snooze
and honey-bees hum
in the heat-haze and a brace
of mallards get their dander up
and a heron tilts on a random
stilt, and when we ease
ourselves around the last
seesawing bend
and Cyprus looms lovely,
we feel as Adam did,
waking to the serene greenery
of Eden.

Rush

There I am halfway
along the cliff-edge
of Georgian Bay, and you
just ahead, eight
years young, hopping
goat-footed and nimble,
as if there wasn't
a steep drop to blue
oblivion, and I felt such
a rush of love I almost
forgot that, should you
fall, I would go
straight down after you,
gulp a thimbleful
of the Deep, and drown.

Buoyancy

On visiting Point Edward: June 2018

What a pleasure it was
to show you the village that un-
wombed me, to cruise Canatara
where I once swam the Summer's
silly and played the days
away at Cowboys and Indians,
and reconnoitre the ells and alleys
where Wiz and the gang made
mischief, and walk again
Grandfather's lawn and point to
the bedroom where I first
pillaged poetry, and meander
the milkweed meadow
a stone's throw from anywhere
and notice that the houses still
lean into their shadows the way
they did when I was barely
a sprout full of bardic dreams,
and what an immeasurable joy
to have shared my boyhood
and its buoyancy with you.

Song

You had a soul that sang
through your blue gaze
and touched the many dozens
who loved you, something
sanguine that was born within you
and thrived for all your days,
and I have such a longing
to have you whole again,
to have you nuzzled next
to me, alive and loving
anew – with your elfin grin,
singing the song of yourself.

Thirty for Anne

When the Dream Ends

I wake and feel the bend
of your body, but when the dream
ends, I am alone in the
condoning dark and you
are still unalive,
but I thank the all-seeing
gods for the tender years
our love thrived and grew
like the incoming rush
of combers on a star-lit
lake and, like larks in the amber
air, we sang the same
home-grown song
and travelled true to the spirit
that bound us beautiful,
and even in death you are
the breath of my being.

Where No Light Goes

You managed to dodge Death
for eighty-three years,
and for five decades of those
we were never apart, your breath
as predictable as the sun licking
a rose with light or a breeze
bullying leaves or a peregrine
hefting Heaven, and now
that you are gone where no
light goes, I'll strive
to remember you: alive and fully
free, your love forever
lodged in my derelict heart.

Alive and Loving

I open my eyes and I am
this side of serenity because
I dreamed you alive and loving
and merely feigning sleep
that morning when I found you
on our green chesterfield,
and I lifted you aloft, your gaze
widening like Lazarua shaking
himself awake, and at ease
in our freedom we strolled
abroad in haphazard unhurry
beside our mutual Lake,
tiptoeing in the rollers
and letting the summer soften
around us, our love un-
shaken, redeemed by a devotion
that would last as long as dreams
abide.

Unforsaken

I wake alone in the
harbouring dark of the room
where our love first bloomed
and hearkened to the song our bodies
sing to themselves
whenever they are tingled
by touch, and I want to hold you
aloft like a beacon-beam
softening in lunar light,
and thank the Venusian gods
who let me love you:
whole-of-heart, righteous,
unforsaken.

Bouquet

That first Christmas,
when our love was nicely new,
I sent you a dozen yellow
roses as a sort of mute
tribute, and it seemed
from that moment on
our passion grew, suffice it
to say, like the slow opening
of those roses, and when
I think of you now
beyond the reach of flowered
affection, I would trade more
than one lifetime
for a chance to close
the gap between us
with the perfumed spray of a
rose bouquet.

Roses

I wake and know you are no
longer a breath away
and that there is an empty
space in the bed where you
let your body be,
and I recall how much
giving you gave to our loving
and I must be content
for your sake with the embers
of whatever I can remember
of those unforgettable
days when love bloomed
like a dozen ripening roses
buzzed by a skein of bees,
and never dreamed that Death
would intervene and leave me
here, grieving for what
once was

Alight

I wake and find you alive
and loving beside me,
your eyes alight in the gloom,
and when I realize I'm still
in the desmesne of dream (knowing
that the gods play us like pawns),
I want to hold you there,
safe and abiding, until
Doomsday dawns.

The Far Side of the Dark

I wake on the far side
of the dark and find you gone
and when I recall the dream
that ferried me through the night,
my heart soars like a lark
rising high in the blue
air and I feel the joy
of a dozen dawns or a whorled
wave breaking, and know
that somewhere in some world
we will share the same star-
harbourng firmament.

Possible

I wake from a dream of you
and I strolling the sands
of Canatara on a summer's
evening mellowed by moon-
light in a sky stippled
with stars blinking news
from the universe onto rollers
below, gentling our toes,
and I take up my pen
and render a rhyme or two
about a world where you
do not die and love is
never lost and everything
is possible.

Tap-Dance

I wake and the moon looms
over our bedroom window
and, behind it, the dark lake
of the sky is back-lit with stars,
and I think of the meandering walks
we took along Doon Pinnacle
with the word "romance" written
on the evening air, and there was
method to my madness when I leaned
over to let your lips marry mine
as our blue eyes harmonized,
and we were more than a stone's
throw away from the day
you left me lingering lonely
while you tap-danced with Death.

Pristine

I wake and brace myself
against the place where
your body lately lay
and I want to take you
by the hand and show you
the village that vaulted me
naked into the world like Adam
nourishing his nudity, his senses
assaulted, and I too
grew a passion for naming,
a penchant for poetry, and if I
could pre-empt you only
for a day, I would sing you sonnets
about the sands of Canatara
and a Lake as pristine as Eden
and sea-breezes to bear
your breath away, and then
I would wish you a happiness
undreamt of in Death.

In the Bone

I wake from a dream of you
and know you are no longer
with me in the irredeemable
dark of the room we once
loved in, and I feel the moon
looming and the shudder of shadow
across the counterpane,
and I try to bring your face
once again into view,
smiling for me alone,
and I yearn for the soothing bruise
of your embrace to ease the brittle
breaking of my heart and the un-
renounceable ache
buried in the bone.

Cruise

You ladled out love as if
there was no end to the gift
of its giving and swathed in the dusting
of moonlight upon
the nuptial bed, you cradled
my lust and made it something
soothing and ceremonial,
and we sent our epithalamium
up to the high Heavens
all the days of our fifty-
seven-year conjugal
cruise.

Soft and Low

Alone at night I sense
your presence in every room
and when I am down, I simply
recall the silken swerve
of your smile or your voice,
like Cordelia's, ever soft
and low or the way you brushed
a curl from your brow or held
horizons in your eyes, and these
small remembrances, these
sweet shudders of delight
touch my heart's core
while your love blooms in my bones
like a sun-rubbed rose.

Ritual

O how you loved a funeral!
tethered to the T.V.
while Jackie wept in black
and Coretta and Bobby grieved,
their dreams sundered by assassins;
you loved the monumental music,
the oomph of the organ, the silk
of ceremony, feelings fuelled
by eulogy, lamentations
of lives lost; you watched
it all, pomp and circumstance,
breathless, moved to tears,
awed by the raw ritual
of death's dance.

Whistle

I see you still in that
lemon frock, behind
the wheel of your silver Volks,
the sun roof flung back
like a wink, and you smile
with the blue beauty of your eyes,
the shock of your hair as ginger
as Rapunzel's unhinged
for her lover, and I cannot find
enough ink to chronicle
the feelings I feel as we jiggle
our joints and whistle off
to Big Town.

Distance

I wake and feel for your presence
beside me, but I am alone
in the nuptial bed, and I try
to recall the blessings of your body,
your breath upon my brow,
your tendrill'd, tremoring touch,
but these whims even now
are vanishing like moonlight
in the morning mist, like the waning
whispers of a dream, and I
confess that our love, so long
in the making and steadier than a
heartbeat is on the ebb-tide,
for Death has too much
distance, its rupture complete.

Tingling

How often have I stood
on Canatara's tingling sands
in the halcyon days of my boy-
hood and watched the sun
set over Huron's horizon,
swathing me in its long,
languid light and rhapsodizing
rollers shaping the shore,
and I want to bring you back
here and show you what
moved me to poetry and delight,
what taught me how to love
something more singular
than myself, something
like the joy you brought singing
into my soul.

Condoning

I wake in the condoning dark,
knowing you are no longer
beside me, and I feel like a
castaway marooned on the moon
in this room where we lay
all the oh-mi-god years
of our loving, and I yearn for the
heft of your breath on my brow
and the tidal tug of your love,
for you are my anchor in a
woe-begone world,
and even now, alone
and bereft, I forgive you your going

Stark

I wake and sense the density
of the dark: the night is moonless
and I am grateful not to see
the place where you would be lying
if the gods were just and the world
worked, and so I close
my eyes and picture you once
again beside me and wonder
how much we trusted to love
and its abiding bloom and how
our happiness grew habitual
as we settled gracefully into our age,
and all was well until the day
you waved goodbye and I felt
the stark stab of your dying.

Oddity

On all those Saturdays
we toddled off to T.O,
I thought of you as a buddy
with a frond of freckles and up-
swept cinnamon locks
and eyes as blue as my brother's
"aggie," but the October day
you drew abreast in your brand-
new Volks and stepped out
into the rarefied air
in your citron frock, my heart
surprised itself and I grew
something more than fond
and felt, for the first time,
the sweet oddity of love.

Still

I loved you best in the
amber afternoons
when we strolled the Doon Pinnacle
hand-in-glove, and in the evenings
we meandered the starlit streets,
mellowed by moonlight,
and I loved you most in the morning
when the sun seeped over
the sill and wished you awake,
and even now, forsaken,
I love you still.

At Ease

I wake and feel the ache
of your absence, and long to return
to the demesne of my dream, where you
are once again beside me,
our room mellowed by moonlight,
and I remember other nights
when our dreams coincided
and we lay in the dappled dark
at ease in one another's
arms, content to live with
the embers of our love, and I hear you
say: "I haven't been this
happy since Eve ate the apple."

Embarcation

I wake in the condoning dark,
desperate for your touch beside me
once again, with moon-
light breaking over the sill,
and once again I summon up
the will to live another
day without you, to find
such solace as I can
in the ache of your absence, wishing
that I could seize on the mysteries
you are now privy to,
that we could come together
in a synchronicity of souls
and embark for the stars.

Big Town

I was the country bumpkin
you took on joyous jaunts
to Big Town and introduced me
to Van Gogh's impassioned
impasto, Mimi's soaring
arias and the exotic haunts
of poets and poetasters,
and bid me sample the alien
tang of Chinese and haute
cuisine, and on the assumption
of my innocence we danced and romanced
our days away, while Death
was just something Hamlet did
to end the play.

Where Love Abides

I wake from a troubled sleep
to feel your presence beside me
once again, s if
you knew I wouldn't make it
on my own, and needed you here
to ease my bereavement pain
and stem the slow drift
into aloneness, and I am
comforted by the familiar furrowing
of the smile you bring to me
now as a gratuitous gift,
and I long to be broken
in your embrace, to be with you
in the places where love abides
and where it burrows deep
int the bone.

No Ending

Last night I dreamt you
alive in every facet
of your loveliness and I have
such memories of our bridal
bed, our bodies blended
in embrace and dappled by moon-
endued shadow, but here
I am in this room
where love once resided,
now emptied of you
and the easing breeze of your touch,
and I want to weave you into
a story as passionate as Eve's
apple-envy, and one with no
ending outside of Eden.

Night After Night

Night after night I see you
in the desmesne of my dreams, and I am
enraptured by the serene gleam
of your smile, and we while away
an hour or two as lovers do
when love is first in bloom,
and I will you no longer
unalive, but thriving here
and now in this room
where we once danced to the demons
of delight and bartered with the
gods of felicity, before
my grief at your going left me
with the fractured fragments
of a heart.

When the Dark is Light Enough

When the dark is light enough,
I see you as you once were
in all your loveliness:
unruffled by Time's tyrannies,
at ease with the world and the wayward
workings of its will, and because
we can find no word
for goodbye, we are pleased
to question Death and its mean
desmesnes and go cruising
moonward, hand-in-glove,
before embarking for the stars.

On Honeymoon Bay

On Honeymoon Bay we lie
in the dark with only the skin
of the tent between us and the stars
and, cradled by the Earth's girth,
we are sung to sleep by the supple
susSuration of wavelets on the beach
below, and when we wake
to make love, I want
to possess you with such
a terrible tenderness, touch
something in you too
deep for words I cannot say,
and teach you how not
to die.

About the Author

Don Gutteridge was born in Sarnia and raised in the nearby village of Point Edward. He taught High School English for seven years, later becoming a Professor in the Faculty of Education at Western University, where he is now Professor Emeritus. He has published seventy-one books: poetry, fiction and scholarly works in literary criticism and pedagogical theory and practice. He has published twenty-two novels, including the twelve-volume Marc Edwards mystery series, and thirty-eight books of poetry, one of which, Coppermine, was short-listed for the 1973 Governor-General's Award. In 1970 he won the UWO President's Medal for the best periodical poem of that year, "Death at Quebec." Don lives in London, Ontario.

To listen to interviews with the author, go to:
http://thereandthen.podbean.com.